Better Homes and Gardens®

LIGHT SALAD MEALS

Our seal assures you that every recipe in *Light Salad Meals*
has been tested in the Better Homes and Gardens® Test Kitchen.
This means that each recipe is practical and reliable, and
meets our high standards of taste appeal.

For years, Better Homes and
Gardens® Books has been
a leader in publishing cook books.
In *Light Salad Meals,* we've pulled
together a delicious collection of
recipes from several of our latest
best-sellers. These no-fail recipes
will make your cooking easier and
more enjoyable.

Editor: Elizabeth Woolever
Editorial Project Manager: Mary Helen Schiltz
Graphic Designer: Harijs Priekulis
Electronic Text Processor: Paula Forest

On the front cover: Fruited Chicken Salad
(see recipe, page 18)

Contents

The Making of à Salad

Proper preparation and freshness—they're the key ingredients in any salad. For hints on preparing salad greens, take a look at these two pages. You'll learn how to handle different greens so they will keep their good quality and flavor.

Cleaning the greens
Clean the greens before storing them. Before washing the greens, remove and discard any outer leaves that are bruised, discolored, tough, or wilted.

Loosen the core from iceberg lettuce by hitting the stem end sharply on a countertop. Then twist the core and lift it out. Don't use a sharp knife to remove the core because the cut edges of iceberg lettuce will turn a rusty color.

Wash iceberg lettuce by placing the core side up under cold running water. Rinse the lettuce thoroughly, then invert the head and let the water run out.

To clean other large-leaf salad greens, such as Bibb lettuce, romaine, and curly endive, cut the bottom core off. Then wash the leaves under cold running water.

Greens with small leaves, such as spinach, watercress, and arugula, should be dunked in a large bowl of cool water. It's important to wash the greens thoroughly

Cleaning

Drying

to remove any dirt and sand particles. After a few minutes, lift the greens out and discard the water. Repeat the dunking of the greens until no more sand collects in the bottom of the bowl.

You'll want to use only the tender leaves from the greens when making a salad. So break off and discard the stems from spinach, Swiss chard, sorrel, and mustard greens; cut out the heavy midrib from romaine; and use only the leaves from arugula and watercress.

Drying the greens
Water on the greens dilutes the salad dressing and prevents the dressing from

basket and then turn the handle to spin the basket. As the basket turns, much of the moisture spins out. But you may still need to blot the leaves dry with a towel.

Crisping and storing greens
If the greens are a little limp, crisp the leaves by putting them in a clear plastic bag while they're still slightly damp. Then refrigerate them for at least eight hours.

Always refrigerate greens until you're ready to use them. When properly stored, greens will stay crisp for as long as three or four days. For most greens, store the leaves in a clear plastic bag or an airtight container.

Tearing greens
Unless a salad calls for shredded lettuce or cabbage, don't cut the greens. Instead, tear the leaves into bite-size pieces. Tearing causes less bruising to the leaves. It also exposes more of the insides of the leaves, which absorb the salad dressing better.

Adding the dressing
A salad dressing should enhance a salad, so add only enough to *lightly* coat the leaves. Too much dressing will mask the other flavors in the salad; too little will leave the salad tasteless.

After the dressing has been added, use two salad servers or spoons to toss the salad.

Crisping and storing

Tearing

Adding the dressing

clinging to the leaves. So after draining the greens, remove as much moisture from them as possible.

An easy way to dry the greens is to place the leaves on paper towels or a clean kitchen towel. Place a second towel over them, then gently pat them dry.

A salad spinner also works well to dry greens. Place small or torn leaves in the

Arugula and watercress need to be stored differently than the other greens. Never store arugula when it's damp because it will turn yellow and rot quickly.

Watercress absorbs water through its stems rather than its leaves. After washing watercress, stand the stems up in a container of water. Cover the leaves loosely with a plastic bag and refrigerate.

Gently push downward to the bottom of the bowl with one salad server and lift up and over with the other server. Don't be too enthusiastic when tossing the salad or you'll bruise the tender leaves.

For arranged salads, you can either drizzle the salad dressing over the top of the arrangement or pass the dressing separately.

Mediterranean Salad

The yogurt in the meatballs adds a flavor bonus.

1 egg
⅓ cup plain yogurt
¾ cup soft bread crumbs
    (1 slice)
½ teaspoon salt
¼ teaspoon ground allspice
1 pound ground beef *or*
    ground lamb
6 cups torn romaine
1½ cups cherry tomatoes,
    halved
1 cup sliced radishes
½ cup sliced green onion
1 2¼-ounce can sliced pitted
    ripe olives, drained
⅓ cup salad oil
¼ cup lemon juice
1 teaspoon dried mint,
    crushed
¼ cup crumbled feta cheese

● In a large mixing bowl beat egg, then add yogurt. Stir in bread crumbs, salt, and allspice. Add ground beef or lamb and mix well. Shape mixture into 1-inch meatballs. Place meatballs in a 15x10x1-inch baking pan.

● Bake, uncovered, in a 350° oven about 15 minutes or till done. Remove meatballs from pan and drain on paper towels. Cool meatballs slightly.

● Meanwhile, in a very large salad bowl combine romaine, tomatoes, radishes, onion, and olives. Cover and chill while preparing dressing. For dressing, in a screw-top jar combine oil, lemon juice, and mint. Cover and shake well.

● For salad, add meatballs to lettuce mixture. Shake dressing again and pour it over lettuce mixture. Toss lightly to coat. Sprinkle salad with feta cheese. Makes 6 servings.

Stir-Fried Beef Salad

Here's a salad you make using a wok.

¾ pound beef round steak
¼ cup clear Italian
    salad dressing
3 cups torn spinach
1 cup sliced fresh mushrooms
1 small cucumber, seeded
    and coarsely chopped
1 large tomato, cut into
    wedges
1 medium onion, sliced and
    separated into rings
½ of a medium green pepper,
    seeded and cut into strips
1 tablespoon cooking oil
⅓ cup clear Italian
    salad dressing

● Trim any excess fat from steak. Partially freeze the steak, then cut on the bias into thin bite-size strips. Place meat in a small mixing bowl.

● Pour the ¼ cup dressing over meat and toss lightly to coat. Let stand at room temperature for 30 minutes.

● In a large salad bowl combine spinach, mushrooms, cucumber, tomato, onion, and green pepper. Cover and chill while cooking the meat.

● Drain meat and discard dressing. Preheat a wok or a large skillet over high heat. Add cooking oil. Stir-fry the meat for 2 to 3 minutes or till brown. Remove from heat.

● Immediately add hot beef and ⅓ cup dressing to spinach mixture. Toss lightly to coat. Makes 4 servings.

Beef and Vegetable Plates

Turn leftover steak into a fresh-tasting, new meal.

¼ cup finely chopped spinach
1 egg yolk
1 tablespoon tarragon vinegar
¼ teaspoon salt
⅛ teaspoon dry mustard
½ cup salad oil
3 to 4 tablespoons milk
12 ounces asparagus
1 pound baby carrots
   Bibb lettuce *or* Boston
   lettuce leaves
8 ounces thinly sliced cooked
   beef, cut into julienne
   strips (about 1½ cups)
3 medium tomatoes, cut into
   wedges
1 small onion, sliced and
   separated into rings

● For dressing, in a blender container combine spinach, egg yolk, tarragon vinegar, salt, and dry mustard. Cover and blend for 10 seconds. Through the opening in the lid or with the lid ajar, and with blender on slow speed, *gradually* add oil in a thin stream. (When necessary, stop the blender and scrape the sides.) Stir in enough of the milk to make dressing of desired consistency. Cover and chill.

● Meanwhile, cut woody base from asparagus. Scrape off scales, then cut spears in half.

● In a large covered saucepan cook carrots in a small amount of lightly salted boiling water for 10 minutes. Add asparagus pieces and continue cooking for 5 to 10 minutes more or till the vegetables are nearly tender, then drain. Rinse with cold water, then drain again. Cover and chill.

● For salads, line 4 salad plates with lettuce leaves. Arrange asparagus, carrots, beef, and tomato wedges in separate piles on the plates, filling surfaces of plates. Top with onion rings. Serve dressing separately. Makes 4 servings.

Beef with Basil Dressing

The rounded edges of the tomato slices and cucumbers form a petallike design.

⅓ cup olive oil *or* salad oil
¼ cup lemon juice
3 tablespoons dry sherry
12 ounces thinly sliced cooked
   beef, cut into julienne
   strips (about 2½ cups)
½ cup thinly sliced green
   onion
½ cup mayonnaise *or* salad
   dressing
1 tablespoon snipped fresh
   basil *or* 1 teaspoon dried
   basil, crushed
2 small tomatoes, halved and
   thinly sliced
1 medium cucumber, thinly
   sliced
2 cups sliced fresh
   mushrooms

● In a medium bowl combine oil, lemon juice, sherry, and ½ teaspoon *salt.* Add beef and onion. Toss lightly to coat. Let stand at room temperature for 20 minutes. Drain beef-onion mixture, reserving 3 tablespoons of the liquid.

● For dressing, in a small mixing bowl combine mayonnaise or salad dressing, basil, and reserved liquid. Stir till well blended.

● For salads, around the outer edges of 4 salad plates, alternately overlap tomato and cucumber slices. (Place rounded edges of tomatoes toward the outer edges of the plates, forming petallike shapes.) Near inner edges of the tomato-cucumber rings, place rings of mushroom slices. Spoon beef mixture into centers of plates. If desired, garnish with fresh basil leaves. Serve dressing separately. Makes 4 servings.

Layered Fiesta Salad

1 15-ounce can garbanzo
    beans, drained
5 cups shredded iceberg
    lettuce *or* torn romaine
2 cups chopped cooked beef
1 medium tomato, seeded and
    chopped
¼ cup sliced pitted ripe olives
¼ cup sliced celery
¼ cup sliced green onion
¾ cup shredded cheddar
    cheese
1 8-ounce carton dairy sour
    cream
1 6-ounce container frozen
    avocado dip, thawed
½ cup milk
½ teaspoon sugar
½ teaspoon chili powder
¼ teaspoon salt
2 tablespoons chopped
    canned green chili
    peppers
1 clove garlic, minced
2 slices bacon, crisp-cooked,
    drained, and crumbled
1 cup crushed tortilla chips

● In a large clear glass salad bowl layer garbanzo beans, lettuce, beef, tomato, olives, celery, onion, and cheese.

● For dressing, in a small mixing bowl combine the sour cream, avocado dip, milk, sugar, chili powder, and salt. Stir till well blended. Stir in green chili peppers and garlic. Spread dressing over top of salad. Cover and chill for up to 24 hours.

● To serve, top with the crumbled bacon. Then sprinkle with tortilla chips. Makes 6 to 8 servings.

Pork and Papaya Salads

¼ cup dried currants
½ cup white wine vinegar
¼ cup walnut oil *or* salad oil
¼ cup chicken broth
1 tablespoon honey
¼ teaspoon ground cinnamon
1 pound cooked boneless pork
    loin roast
1 head Belgian endive
    Bibb lettuce leaves
2 papayas, seeded, peeled, and
    sliced lengthwise
2 avocados, seeded, peeled,
    and sliced lengthwise
¼ cup broken walnuts

● In a small bowl pour enough boiling *water* over currants to cover. Let stand for 5 minutes, then drain.

● For dressing, in a screw-top jar combine vinegar, oil, chicken broth, honey, and cinnamon. Cover and shake well.

● For salads, trim fat from pork roast and slice thinly. Separate leaves of Belgian endive. Line 6 salad plates with Bibb lettuce leaves. Arrange pork, Belgian endive, papaya, and avocado on the plates. Sprinkle with currants and walnuts. Drizzle the dressing evenly over salads. If desired, garnish with julienne strips of lime peel. Makes 6 servings.

Pork and Papaya Salads

Taco Salad

Here are all the makings of a taco—a tortilla, beef, cheese, and lettuce—in a meal-size salad.

Tortilla Bowls
¾ pound lean ground beef
½ cup chopped onion
1 clove garlic, minced
1 cup canned whole kernel corn
1 8-ounce can tomato sauce
1 7½-ounce can tomatoes, cut up
1 4-ounce can green chili peppers, rinsed, seeded, and chopped
1 tablespoon all-purpose flour
2 teaspoons chili powder
6 cups torn lettuce
1 cup shredded cheddar *or* American cheese
¼ cup sliced pitted ripe olives
1 tomato, cut into wedges
1 green pepper, cut into strips

● Prepare Tortilla Bowls; cool. Remove foil from bowls.
● Cook ground beef, chopped onion, and garlic till meat is browned and onion is tender; drain well. Stir in drained corn, tomato sauce, *undrained* tomatoes, green chili peppers, flour, and chili powder. Cook and stir till thickened and bubbly. Cook and stir 1 minute more.
● Meanwhile, combine lettuce, ¾ *cup* of the shredded cheese, and the ripe olives; toss lightly. Place lettuce mixture in Tortilla Bowls. Spoon meat mixture over lettuce mixture.
● Top each salad with tomato wedges and green pepper strips. Sprinkle with remaining cheese. Makes 4 servings.

Tortilla Bowls: Cut eight 10-inch circles from heavy-duty foil. In a large skillet warm four 10-inch *flour tortillas,* one at a time, over low heat about 1 minute or just till warm and pliable. Place *each* warm tortilla on 2 foil circles and shape into a ruffled bowl. Place tortilla bowls on an ungreased baking sheet. Bake in a 350° oven about 10 minutes or till crisp.

Making Tortilla Bowls
Put the lid of a 10-inch skillet on top of eight sheets of heavy-duty foil. Draw around lid, forming a 10-inch circle. Holding foil sheets together, cut out circle.

Warm the tortillas, one at a time, in a skillet over low heat. Heat about one minute or just till warm and pliable.

Put two foil circles together; top with warm tortilla. Shape tortilla and foil together into a ruffled bowl. Repeat with remaining foil circles and tortillas. (The foil acts as a support.)

Place tortilla bowls on an ungreased baking sheet. Bake in a 350° oven about 10 minutes or till crisp. Cool; remove foil. Fill with salad.

Vegetable-Ham Medley Salad

A salad so colorful you can skip the garnish.

1 cup fresh *or* frozen peas
2 cups cooked rice
1 cup cubed fully cooked ham
  or cooked pork
4 ounces cheddar cheese,
  cubed
¾ cup chopped celery
½ cup chopped green pepper
2 tablespoons snipped chives
  or green onion tops
3 tablespoons white wine
  vinegar
3 tablespoons olive oil *or*
  salad oil
1½ teaspoons snipped fresh
  basil *or* chervil, *or*
  ½ teaspoon dried basil
  or chervil, crushed
  Leaf lettuce

● In a small covered saucepan cook fresh peas in a small amount of lightly salted boiling water about 5 minutes or till tender, then drain. (Or cook frozen peas according to package directions, then drain.) Rinse with cold water, then drain again.

● In a medium mixing bowl combine the cooked peas, rice, ham or pork, cheese, celery, green pepper, and chives or green onion tops. Toss lightly to mix. Cover and chill till serving time.

● For dressing, in a screw-top jar combine vinegar, oil, basil or chervil, ¼ teaspoon *salt,* and ⅛ teaspoon *pepper.* Cover and shake well. Chill till serving time.

● To serve, shake dressing and pour it over rice mixture. Toss lightly to coat. Line 4 salad plates with lettuce leaves. Spoon rice mixture onto the plates. Makes 4 servings.

Cheese Macaroni Salad

Surprise! Use a simple macaroni-and-cheese dinner mix as the base for this pasta salad.

1 7¼-ounce package
  macaroni-and-
  cheese dinner mix
1 9-ounce package frozen
  Italian green beans
1½ cups milk
1½ teaspoons dried basil,
  crushed
8 ounces fully cooked ham,
  cut into bite-size julienne
  strips (about 1½ cups)
½ cup pitted ripe olives, halved
½ cup dairy sour cream
½ cup mayonnaise *or* salad
  dressing
2 tablespoons snipped parsley
1 tablespoon Dijon-style
  mustard
⅛ teaspoon onion powder
  Romaine leaves
  Small tomato wedges

● In a large saucepan cook macaroni from dinner mix in 6 cups boiling *water* for 5 minutes. Add beans and return to boiling. Boil gently, covered, for 4 to 5 minutes more or till macaroni and beans are tender. Drain.

● Stir cheese sauce mix from dinner mix, milk, and basil into macaroni and beans in saucepan. Cook over medium heat about 5 minutes or till slightly thickened and bubbly. Cook and stir for 1 minute more. Remove from heat and cool slightly, stirring once or twice.

● In a large mixing bowl combine macaroni mixture, ham, and olives. In a small mixing bowl stir together sour cream, mayonnaise or salad dressing, parsley, mustard, and onion powder. Pour sour cream mixture over macaroni mixture. Toss lightly to coat. Cover and chill the mixture for 6 hours or overnight.

● To serve, if necessary, stir in several tablespoons of additional *milk* to moisten mixture. Line 4 salad plates with lettuce leaves. Spoon macaroni mixture onto the plates. Garnish with tomato wedges. Makes 4 servings.

Create-a-Chef's Salad

Create your own salad by choosing your favorite luncheon meat and dressing.

3 cups torn iceberg lettuce
3 cups torn romaine
2 tomatoes, cut into wedges
1½ cups desired cold cuts cut into julienne strips
4 ounces American, cheddar, *or* Swiss cheese, cubed
½ of a small cucumber, sliced
½ of a small red onion, sliced and separated into rings
½ of a green pepper, cut into rings
3 hard-cooked eggs, sliced
Desired salad dressing

● In a very large mixing bowl combine iceberg lettuce, romaine, tomatoes, meat, cheese, cucumber, onion, and green pepper. Toss lightly to mix.

● To serve, spoon lettuce mixture onto 6 salad plates. Garnish with egg slices. Serve with desired salad dressing. Serves 6.

Deli-Style Pasta Salad

1 7-ounce package corkscrew macaroni
6 ounces provolone cheese, cut into ¾-inch cubes
6 ounces sliced Genoa salami, cut into strips
1 small zucchini, thinly sliced
1 small onion, thinly sliced and separated into rings
½ cup chopped green pepper *or* sweet red pepper
1 2¼-ounce can sliced pitted ripe olives, drained
¼ cup grated Parmesan cheese
¼ cup snipped parsley
½ cup olive oil
¼ cup white wine vinegar
1½ teaspoons dry mustard
1 teaspoon dried oregano, crushed
1 teaspoon dried basil, crushed
1 clove garlic, minced
2 medium tomatoes, cut into wedges
Parsley sprigs (optional)

● Cook macaroni according to package directions, then drain. Rinse with cold water, then drain again.

● In a large mixing bowl combine macaroni, provolone cheese, salami, zucchini, onion, green or red pepper, olives, Parmesan cheese, and snipped parsley.

● For dressing, in a screw-top jar combine olive oil, vinegar, dry mustard, oregano, basil, and garlic. Cover and shake well. Pour dressing over pasta mixture and toss lightly to coat. Cover and chill for 4 hours or overnight.

● To serve, add tomato wedges and toss lightly. Transfer pasta mixture to a large salad bowl. If desired, garnish with parsley sprigs. Makes 8 servings.

Deli-Style Pasta Salad

Asparagus-Brats Toss

This recipe has all the makings of the perfect potluck food—it's easy to tote and can be made up to 24 hours ahead.

4 ounces spaghetti
½ teaspoon dried basil, crushed
½ teaspoon dried thyme, crushed
10 ounces fresh asparagus, *or* one 8- *or* 10-ounce package frozen cut asparagus
12 ounces cooked bratwurst, bias-sliced into ¼-inch slices
2 small tomatoes, cut into wedges
¼ cup sliced green onion
½ cup creamy Italian salad dressing
Milk
Grated Parmesan cheese

● Break spaghetti into 2-inch-long pieces. Cook the spaghetti according to package directions, then drain. Rinse with cold water, then drain again. Place spaghetti in a large salad bowl. Add basil and thyme, then toss lightly to mix. Set mixture aside.

● Cut fresh asparagus into 1-inch pieces. In a medium covered saucepan cook fresh asparagus in a small amount of lightly salted boiling water for 8 to 10 minutes or till nearly tender, then drain. (Or cook frozen asparagus according to package directions, then drain.) Rinse with cold water. Drain again.

● Add asparagus, bratwurst, tomatoes, and green onion to spaghetti mixture. Pour dressing over spaghetti mixture and toss lightly to coat. Cover and chill for 3 to 24 hours.

● To serve, if necessary, add a few tablespoons of milk and toss spaghetti mixture lightly to moisten mixture. Sprinkle with Parmesan cheese. Makes 4 servings.

Hot Potato and Bratwurst Salad

Here's a Test Kitchen tip: If tiny new potatoes are unavailable, cube three medium potatoes and cook them for 10 to 15 minutes in the lightly salted boiling water.

1 pound whole tiny new potatoes, each cut into eight wedges
2 slices bacon
12 ounces smoked bratwurst *or* knackwurst, bias-sliced into ¼-inch slices
⅓ cup chopped onion
¼ cup sliced celery
1 tablespoon sugar
1½ teaspoons cornstarch
¼ teaspoon salt
¼ teaspoon celery seed
Dash pepper
⅓ cup water
3 tablespoons vinegar
Snipped parsley

● In a large covered saucepan cook potatoes in lightly salted boiling water for 8 to 10 minutes or just till tender. Drain the potatoes and set aside.

● In a 10-inch skillet cook bacon till crisp. Remove bacon from skillet, reserving 1 tablespoon drippings. Crumble bacon and set aside. In the skillet cook bratwurst or knackwurst, onion, and celery in the reserved drippings till meat is light brown and vegetables are tender, stirring occasionally.

● In a small mixing bowl combine the sugar, cornstarch, salt, celery seed, and pepper. Stir in water and vinegar. Pour over bratwurst mixture in skillet. Cook and stir till thickened and bubbly. Add the potatoes and bacon. Continue cooking for 3 to 5 minutes more or till potatoes are heated through, tossing lightly to coat. Sprinkle with parsley. Makes 4 servings.

Salad-Making Hints

What's a Cup?

Most ingredients in our recipes call for cup measures. But when you're shopping, how much should you buy? Here's a guide to help you in your planning.

Ingredient	Amount Before Preparation	Approximate Measure After Preparation
Bibb lettuce	1 medium head (5 ounces)	3 cups torn
Boston lettuce	1 medium head (8 ounces)	5 cups torn
Broccoli	1 pound	3½ cups flowerets
Cabbage	1 small head (1 pound)	5 cups shredded
Carrots	2 medium (5 ounces)	1 cup sliced
Cauliflower	1 medium head (1½ pounds)	4 cups flowerets
Celery	1 stalk	½ cup sliced
Cheese	4 ounces	1 cup shredded
Cucumber	1 medium (8 ounces)	1¾ cups sliced *or* 1¼ cups chopped
Green onions with tops	1 bunch (7 medium)	½ cup sliced
Green pepper	1 large	1 cup chopped
Iceberg lettuce	1 small head (15 ounces)	7½ cups torn *or* 8 cups shredded
Meat, cooked	1 pound	3 cups chopped
Mushrooms	16 large (8 ounces)	3 cups sliced
Radishes	12 medium (4 ounces)	1 cup sliced
Romaine	1 medium head (1 pound)	10 cups torn
Sorrel	4 ounces	5½ cups torn
Spinach	1 pound	12 cups torn
Tomato	1 medium (6 ounces)	1 cup chopped
Watercress	4 ounces	2 cups leaves only
Zucchini	1 medium (8 ounces)	2 cups sliced

Sparkling Strawberry-and-Poultry Salad

Jicamas (HEE-kuh-muhs), of Mexican origin, resemble turnips in shape but have a delicate flavor like water chestnuts.

8 cups torn spinach
2 cups sliced strawberries
8 ounces cooked chicken, cut into bite-size pieces (about 1½ cups)
5 ounces jicama, peeled and cut into 2-inch julienne sticks (about 1 cup), *or* one 8-ounce can sliced water chestnuts, drained
⅓ cup apricot nectar
¼ cup salad oil
2 tablespoons red wine vinegar *or* Raspberry-Mint Vinegar (see recipe, page 44)
¼ teaspoon sesame oil
¼ cup slivered almonds, toasted

● In a very large salad bowl combine the spinach, strawberries, chicken, and jicama or water chestnuts. Cover and chill while preparing the dressing.

● For dressing, in a screw-top jar combine apricot nectar, salad oil, vinegar, and sesame oil. Cover and shake well. Pour dressing over spinach mixture and toss lightly to coat. Sprinkle with almonds. Makes 4 servings.

Chicken-Spinach Salad

A salad with a delightful contrast—slightly sweet from the dressing and slightly bitter from the radicchio (rah-DEE-kee-oh).

3 cups torn spinach
1 cup torn radicchio *or* shredded red cabbage
5 ounces cooked chicken *or* turkey, cut into bite-size pieces (1 cup)
¼ of a small onion, thinly sliced and separated into rings
3 tablespoons salad oil
2 tablespoons cider vinegar
2 teaspoons brown sugar
2 slices bacon, crisp-cooked, drained, and crumbled
1 hard-cooked egg, chopped

● In a large mixing bowl combine spinach, radicchio or red cabbage, chicken or turkey, and onion. Cover and chill while preparing the dressing.

● For dressing, in a small bowl combine oil, vinegar, and sugar. Stir till sugar is dissolved. Pour dressing over spinach mixture and toss lightly to coat.

● To serve, spoon spinach mixture onto 2 plates. Sprinkle with crumbled bacon and chopped egg. Makes 2 servings.

Chicken-Spinach Salad

Fruited Chicken Salad

Pictured on the cover.

⅔ cup mayonnaise *or* salad dressing
2 tablespoons brown mustard
1 tablespoon brown sugar
1 clove garlic, minced
1 11-ounce can mandarin orange sections, drained
1 15¼-ounce can pineapple slices (juice pack), drained
4 cups cubed cooked chicken
1 cup thinly sliced celery
½ cup chopped green pepper
  Romaine leaves *and/or* leaf lettuce

● For dressing, in a small mixing bowl combine mayonnaise or salad dressing, mustard, sugar, and garlic. Stir till well blended. Cover and chill.

● Meanwhile, reserve several orange sections for garnish. Quarter the pineapple slices. In a large mixing bowl combine remaining orange sections, pineapple, chicken, celery, and green pepper. If desired, cover and chill for up to 4 hours.

● For salad, pour the dressing over the chicken mixture. Toss mixture lightly to coat.

● To serve, line 4 to 6 plates with romaine leaves and/or leaf lettuce. Transfer chicken mixture to the plates. Garnish with the reserved orange sections. Makes 4 to 6 servings.

Fennel-Chicken Salad

Looking for a great way to use up leftover chicken or turkey? Marinate it in wine vinegar, fennel, and rosemary for a sensational flavor.

⅓ cup olive oil *or* salad oil
¼ cup white wine vinegar
¼ teaspoon fennel seed, crushed
¼ teaspoon dried rosemary, crushed
  Several drops bottled hot pepper sauce
2½ cups cubed cooked chicken *or* turkey
1½ cups sliced cauliflower *or* broccoli flowerets
3 medium plums, pitted and sliced, *or* one 8½-ounce can whole unpitted purple plums, drained, pitted, and sliced
½ cup sliced radishes
4 cups shredded Chinese cabbage
¾ cup cashews

● In a medium salad bowl combine oil, wine vinegar, fennel, rosemary, hot pepper sauce, and ¼ teaspoon *salt*. Add chicken or turkey, cauliflower or broccoli, plums, and radishes. Toss lightly to coat. Cover and chill for 2 hours.

● To serve, stir mixture in bowl. Add the Chinese cabbage and cashews. Toss lightly to mix. Makes 6 servings.

Wilted Lettuce with Chicken

"It's more than just a wilted salad," commented one of the editors on the taste panel. Chicken, apples, and mushrooms turn this lettuce salad into a hearty meal.

3 cups torn romaine
3 cups torn red leaf lettuce
1 cup sliced fresh mushrooms
¼ cup sliced green onion
1 tablespoon olive oil *or* cooking oil
1 whole large chicken breast (1 pound), skinned, boned, and cut into bite-size julienne strips
1 teaspoon mustard seed
3 tablespoons olive oil *or* cooking oil
2 tablespoons white wine vinegar
2 small apples, cut into very thin wedges
3 hard-cooked eggs, cut into wedges

● In a large mixing bowl combine romaine, leaf lettuce, mushrooms, and onion. Toss lightly to mix. Set lettuce mixture aside.

● In a 12-inch skillet heat the 1 tablespoon oil over medium-high heat. Add chicken and mustard seed, then cook and stir for 2 to 3 minutes or till chicken is tender. Reduce heat to medium.

● Stir in the 3 tablespoons oil and vinegar. Add apples, and cook and stir for 30 seconds. Remove skillet from heat. Immediately add the lettuce mixture and carefully toss about 1 minute or till lettuce begins to wilt. Spoon the lettuce mixture onto 4 salad plates. Garnish with egg wedges. Makes 4 servings.

Wilting lettuce
After cooking the apples, remove the skillet from the heat. Immediately add the lettuce mixture to the hot dressing in the skillet. Then carefully toss the lettuce with the dressing for 1 minute or until the lettuce begins to wilt and is no longer crisp, as shown. The lettuce wilts because of the heat from the dressing and the skillet.

Spoon the mixture onto salad plates and garnish with hard-cooked egg wedges. Serve the salad while the lettuce is still warm.

Lemony Chicken-and-Broccoli Salad

For a light and refreshing look, use only the white meat from the chicken.

¾ pound broccoli
12 ounces cooked chicken, cut
    into julienne strips
    (about 2½ cups)
1½ cups sliced fresh
    mushrooms
½ cup mayonnaise *or* salad
    dressing
½ cup plain yogurt
1 tablespoon milk
¼ teaspoon finely shredded
    lemon peel
    Dash salt
    Dash pepper
    Dash Worcestershire sauce
    Milk
¼ cup toasted pine nuts *or*
    sliced almonds, toasted
    Romaine leaves

● Remove outer leaves and tough parts of stalks from the broccoli. Cut the broccoli stalks crosswise into ¼-inch-thick slices, then break the flowerets into smaller pieces. (You should have about 4 cups total.)

● In a medium covered saucepan cook broccoli in a small amount of lightly salted boiling water for 4 to 5 minutes or till nearly tender, then drain. Rinse with cold water. Drain again. In a mixing bowl combine the broccoli, chicken, and mushrooms.

● For dressing, in a small mixing bowl combine mayonnaise or salad dressing, yogurt, 1 tablespoon milk, lemon peel, salt, pepper, and Worcestershire sauce. Stir till well blended. Pour the dressing over broccoli mixture and toss lightly to coat. Cover and chill the mixture for 4 to 6 hours.

● To serve, if necessary, stir in a few tablespoons of additional milk to moisten mixture. Add nuts and toss lightly to mix. Line a medium salad bowl with lettuce leaves. Transfer the broccoli mixture to the bowl. Makes 4 servings.

Slim Chicken Slaw

You can make this low-calorie salad up to 6 hours before serving.

1 tablespoon all-purpose flour
1 tablespoon sugar
½ teaspoon salt
½ teaspoon dry mustard
½ teaspoon celery seed
½ cup skim milk
1 slightly beaten egg yolk
1 tablespoon vinegar
1 tablespoon lemon juice
3 cups shredded cabbage
2 cups chopped cooked
    chicken breast *or* turkey
    breast
1 cup seedless red grapes,
    halved
½ cup sliced celery
½ cup chopped walnuts

● For dressing, in a small saucepan combine flour, sugar, salt, dry mustard, and celery seed. Gradually stir in milk. Cook and stir over medium heat till thickened and bubbly. Stir *half* of the hot mixture into the beaten egg yolk, then return all to saucepan. Cook and stir over low heat for 1 to 2 minutes more or till thickened. Stir in vinegar and lemon juice, then cool mixture.

● In a medium salad bowl combine cabbage, chicken or turkey, grapes, celery, and walnuts. Pour cooled dressing over cabbage mixture and toss lightly to coat. Cover and chill for 2 to 6 hours. Makes 4 servings.

Chicken Pocket Sandwiches

Use the tines of a fork to carefully open a pita bread half into a "pocket."

2 cups chopped cabbage
1½ cups chopped cooked chicken
1 cup shredded carrot
½ cup broken walnuts
¼ cup chopped radish
⅓ cup mayonnaise *or* salad dressing
⅓ cup plain yogurt
2 tablespoons milk
1 tablespoon Dijon-style mustard
⅛ teaspoon salt
3 large whole wheat pita bread rounds, halved crosswise
½ cup shredded cheddar cheese

● In a large mixing bowl combine cabbage, chicken, carrot, walnuts, and radish.

● For dressing, in a small mixing bowl combine mayonnaise or salad dressing, yogurt, milk, mustard, and salt. Stir till well blended. Pour dressing over cabbage mixture and toss lightly to coat. If desired, cover and chill for up to 5 hours.

● To serve, stir cabbage mixture. Spoon mixture into bread halves. Sprinkle with cheese. Makes 3 servings.

Chicken Salad Tacos

A twist to the typical taco! Chicken salad made with sour cream, avocado, olives, and seasonings gives this version a great Mexican flavor.

⅓ cup mayonnaise *or* salad dressing
⅓ cup dairy sour cream *or* plain yogurt
2 tablespoons chopped onion
2 tablespoons snipped cilantro *or* parsley
1 tablespoon lime juice
2 teaspoons taco seasoning mix
2½ cups chopped cooked chicken *or* turkey
2 medium tomatoes, seeded and chopped
¼ cup sliced pitted ripe olives
1½ cups finely shredded iceberg lettuce
10 taco shells
1 avocado, seeded, peeled, and sliced lengthwise

● In a medium mixing bowl combine mayonnaise or salad dressing, sour cream or yogurt, onion, cilantro or parsley, lime juice, and taco seasoning. Stir in chicken or turkey, tomatoes, and olives. If desired, cover and chill for up to 4 hours.

● To serve, place some lettuce in each taco shell. Spoon chicken mixture on top of lettuce in the shells. Garnish with avocado slices. Makes 5 servings.

Chicken, Shrimp, and Fruit Salad

Since fresh cantaloupe and honeydew melon are in season at the same time, alternate using one or the other in this main-dish salad.

2 cups cubed cooked chicken *or* turkey
1 cup seedless green grapes, halved
1 cup cubed cantaloupe *or* honeydew melon
1 8-ounce can sliced water chestnuts, drained
1 4½-ounce can shrimp, rinsed and drained
1 small banana
⅓ cup mayonnaise *or* salad dressing
1 tablespoon lemon juice
   Lettuce leaves (optional)

● For salad, in a large bowl combine cooked chicken or turkey, halved grapes, cubed cantaloupe or honeydew melon, water chestnuts, and shrimp. Cover and chill for several hours.

● For dressing, in a small bowl mash the banana. Stir in the mayonnaise or salad dressing and the lemon juice. Cover; chill for several hours.

● If desired, arrange lettuce leaves on plates. Serve salad atop lettuce. Drizzle with dressing. Makes 6 servings.

Chicken-Sesame Salad

The radishes add crispness to the salad, as well as a peppery flavor.

2 tablespoons salad oil
2 tablespoons vinegar
1 tablespoon sesame seed, toasted
1 teaspoon sugar
¼ teaspoon salt
⅛ teaspoon pepper
4 cups torn salad greens
2 cups cooked chicken *or* turkey, cut into bite-size strips
5 radishes, sliced
2 green onions, sliced
1 hard-cooked egg, cut into wedges

● For dressing, in a screw-top jar combine salad oil, vinegar, sesame seed, sugar, salt, and pepper. Cover and shake well to mix. Chill thoroughly.

● For salad, in a large salad bowl combine torn salad greens, cooked chicken or turkey, sliced radishes, and sliced green onions. Toss lightly.

● Shake dressing again just before serving. Pour dressing over salad; toss lightly to coat. Garnish with the hard-cooked egg wedges. Makes 4 servings.

Chicken, Shrimp, and
Fruit Salad

Chicken-Avocado Salad

Chilling the salad and dressing separately prevents the rice in the salad from absorbing too much of the dressing.

3 cups cooked rice
3 cups chopped cooked
   chicken
½ cup thinly sliced celery
¼ cup thinly sliced green
   onion
1 medium avocado
⅓ cup mayonnaise *or* salad
   dressing
¼ cup milk
2 tablespoons vinegar
1 teaspoon dried parsley
   flakes
⅛ teaspoon salt
   Lettuce leaves
   Avocado slices (optional)
   Tomato wedges (optional)

● In a large bowl combine the cooked rice, chopped chicken, sliced celery, and sliced green onion. Cover the rice mixture; chill for several hours.

● Use a sharp knife to cut the avocado in half lengthwise. Twist the avocado gently to separate the two halves. Tap the seed with the blade of the knife so the blade remains in the seed. Twist and gently lift out the seed. Use the sharp knife to peel the halved avocado.

● For the dressing, mash the avocado pulp. Stir in the mayonnaise or salad dressing, milk, vinegar, parsley flakes, and salt. Cover and chill for several hours.

● Just before serving, pour the dressing over the rice mixture; toss lightly to coat. Arrange lettuce leaves on plates. Serve the salad atop lettuce. Garnish with avocado slices and tomato wedges, if desired. Makes 6 servings.

How to "Julienne"

In many salad recipes, you'll notice that some of the ingredients need to be cut into "julienne strips." Just what is this cut and how do you do it?

To "julienne" meats and vegetables means to cut them into long thin strips.

Start by cutting a thin slice off one side of the meat or vegetable, if necessary, so it will lie flat on the cutting surface. Placing the flat side down, cut the food into lengthwise slices. Then cut each slice into narrow strips about ⅛ to ¼ inch thick.

Selecting and preparing an avocado

For best flavor, an avocado must be ripe before you use it in this salad. To test ripeness, cradle the avocado in the palm of your hand; if it yields to gentle pressure, it's ready to use. If some feeling of firmness remains, however, keep the avocado at room temperature till it reaches the desired softness. You may store a ripe avocado in the refrigerator for up to three days.

To prepare the avocado, cut the fruit lengthwise around the seed. Gently twist the halves in opposite directions to separate.

To remove the seed from the avocado, carefully tap the seed with the blade of a sharp knife so the blade is caught in the seed. Rotate the knife to loosen the seed, then use the knife to lift the seed out. (This method of removing the seed lessens the bruising of the avocado.)

To peel the avocado, place the cut side down in your palm. Use the sharp knife to loosen and strip the skin from the fruit.

Chicken Salad on Melon

Melon, strawberries, and poppy seed dressing spell S-C-R-U-M-P-T-I-O-U-S-!

2 tablespoons sugar
2 tablespoons vinegar
1 tablespoon lemon juice
⅛ teaspoon dry mustard
    Dash salt
¼ cup salad oil
¼ teaspoon poppy seed
1½ cups cubed cooked chicken
    or turkey
¼ of a medium cantaloupe
¼ of a medium honeydew
    melon
2 Bibb lettuce *or* Boston
    lettuce cups
1 cup strawberries, quartered
½ cup walnut halves
    Whole strawberries

● For dressing, in a blender container combine sugar, vinegar, lemon juice, dry mustard, and salt. Cover and blend for 5 seconds. Through the opening in the lid or with lid ajar, and with the blender on slow speed, *gradually* add oil in a thin stream. (When necessary, stop blender and scrape sides.) Cover and blend for 1 to 2 minutes more or till the dressing is slightly thickened. Stir in poppy seed.

● In a medium mixing bowl pour the dressing over chicken or turkey. Toss lightly to coat. Cover and chill for 30 to 45 minutes.

● Meanwhile, remove seeds from cantaloupe and honeydew melon. Peel melons and slice pulp lengthwise into ¼-inch-thick slices. Cover and chill.

● For salads, place lettuce cups in centers of 2 salad plates. Alternately overlap cantaloupe and honeydew melon slices around the lettuce cups, forming rings. Add 1 cup strawberries and walnuts to chicken mixture, then toss lightly to coat. Spoon chicken mixture into lettuce cups. Garnish with the whole strawberries. Makes 2 servings.

Gourmet's Delight

Look for the smoked turkey breast at the deli.

½ cup peach yogurt
1 3-ounce package cream
    cheese, softened
4 medium peaches, pears, *or*
    nectarines; *or* 8 small
    apricots; *or* 4 kiwi fruits
    Bibb lettuce *or* Boston
    lettuce leaves
12 ounces fully cooked smoked
    turkey breast, turkey
    roast, *or* ham, sliced
¼ cup chopped macadamia
    nuts, pistachio nuts,
    or cashews

● For dressing, in a small mixer bowl combine yogurt and cream cheese. Beat with an electric mixer on medium speed till well blended. Cover and chill.

● If necessary, peel the fruit. Then slice it.

● For salads, line 4 salad plates with lettuce leaves. From the tops to the bottoms of the plates, overlap slices of turkey or ham. Then slightly overlap fruit slices on meat. Spoon dressing over top of each salad. Sprinkle with nuts. Makes 4 servings.

Chicken 'n' Walnut Puff

One BIG cream puff shell filled with a tarragon chicken salad.

1 cup water
½ cup butter *or* margarine
1 cup all-purpose flour
4 eggs
3 cups shredded Chinese cabbage
2 cups finely chopped cooked chicken
¾ cup broken walnuts
⅓ cup shredded carrot
¼ cup thinly sliced green onion
⅔ cup mayonnaise *or* salad dressing
½ cup dairy sour cream
2 tablespoons vinegar
½ teaspoon dried tarragon, crushed
2 small cloves garlic, minced
½ of a 6-ounce package (about 1 cup) frozen pea pods, thawed (optional)

● For puff shell, in a medium saucepan bring water to boiling. Reduce heat. Add the butter or margarine and stir till melted. Add flour and ¼ teaspoon *salt* all at once, stirring vigorously. Cook and stir till the mixture forms a ball that doesn't separate. Remove from heat and cool slightly, about 5 minutes.

● Add eggs, 1 at a time, beating after each addition till smooth. Spread batter over the bottom and up the sides of a greased 10-inch pie plate or quiche dish. Bake in a 400° oven for 25 to 30 minutes or till golden brown and puffy. Leave the puff shell in the pie plate and cool it on a wire rack.

● Meanwhile, for salad mixture, in a large mixing bowl combine Chinese cabbage, chicken, walnuts, carrot, and onion.

● For dressing, in a small mixing bowl combine mayonnaise or salad dressing, sour cream, vinegar, tarragon, garlic, and ⅛ teaspoon *salt*. Stir till well blended. Pour over salad mixture. Toss lightly to coat. If desired, cover and chill for 30 minutes.

● To serve, spoon salad mixture into the puff shell. If desired, garnish with pea pods. Cut into wedges. Makes 6 servings.

Papaya Boats with Chicken

You choose: Either remove the peels from the papayas or leave them on.

2 papayas
3 cups chopped cooked chicken
2 tablespoons thinly sliced green onion
1 8-ounce carton dairy sour cream
2 tablespoons frozen orange juice concentrate, thawed
1 tablespoon snipped cilantro *or* 1 teaspoon ground coriander
½ teaspoon dry mustard
2 drops bottled hot pepper sauce
2 cups shredded iceberg lettuce (optional)
¼ cup coconut, toasted

● For papaya shells, use a sharp knife to cut the papayas lengthwise in half. Remove seeds. Cut out papaya pulp, leaving ¼-inch-thick shells. Cover and chill shells.

● Cut papaya pulp into ½-inch cubes. In a medium mixing bowl combine cubed papaya, chicken, and green onion.

● For the dressing, in a small mixing bowl combine sour cream, orange juice concentrate, cilantro or coriander, dry mustard, and hot pepper sauce. Stir till well blended. Pour dressing over chicken mixture. Toss lightly to coat. If desired, cover and chill the chicken mixture for up to 4 hours.

● To serve, if desired, arrange lettuce on 4 salad plates. Place the papaya shells onto the lettuce. Spoon chicken mixture into papaya shells. Sprinkle with toasted coconut. If desired, garnish with cilantro or parsley sprigs. Makes 4 servings.

Tossed Cusk Salad with Lemon-Mustard Dressing

½ cup mayonnaise *or* salad
    dressing
1 teaspoon finely shredded
    lemon peel
1 tablespoon lemon juice
2 teaspoons Dijon-style
    mustard
    Dash garlic powder
¼ cup whipping cream
1 pound chilled cooked cusk,
    cod, flounder, *or* orange
    roughy
4 cups torn Bibb lettuce *or*
    Boston lettuce
1 cup torn sorrel *or* spinach
1 cup cherry tomatoes, halved
1 cup sliced fresh mushrooms
2 tablespoons capers, drained

● For the dressing, in a small mixing bowl stir together the mayonnaise or salad dressing, lemon peel, juice, mustard, and garlic. In another small bowl whip cream till soft peaks form. Then fold whipped cream into mayonnaise mixture. If necessary, stir in 1 to 2 tablespoons *milk* to make dressing of desired consistency. Cover and chill dressing while preparing salad.

● For the salad, break or cut the fish into large chunks. (You should have about 2⅔ cups.) In a large mixing bowl combine the fish, lettuce, sorrel or spinach, cherry tomatoes, and mushrooms. Toss lightly to mix.

● To serve, spoon lettuce mixture onto salad plates. Drizzle with dressing. Sprinkle with capers. Makes 4 servings.

Fresh Tuna Salade Niçoise

1½ cups cut fresh green beans
½ pound whole tiny new
    potatoes (4 to 6)
1 cup olive oil *or* salad oil
½ cup white wine vinegar
1 tablespoon dry mustard
1 tablespoon capers, drained
    and chopped (optional)
1 teaspoon dried basil,
    crushed
1 teaspoon dried oregano,
    crushed
2 cloves garlic, minced
12 ounces cooked tuna
1 medium green pepper, cut
    into strips
1 cup cherry tomatoes, halved
¾ cup pitted ripe olives
2 cups torn romaine
2 cups torn Bibb lettuce *or*
    Boston lettuce
½ of a 2-ounce can anchovy
    fillets, drained and halved

● In a medium covered saucepan cook fresh beans in lightly salted boiling water for 10 minutes, then carefully add potatoes and return to boiling. Continue cooking about 15 minutes more or till vegetables are nearly tender, then drain. Rinse with cold water and drain again.

● Meanwhile, for the dressing, in a screw-top jar combine the oil, vinegar, dry mustard, capers (if desired), basil, oregano, and minced garlic. Cover and shake well.

● Break or cut tuna into large chunks. (You should have about 2 cups.) Place tuna in a dish just large enough to hold the fish in a single layer. Pour ½ *cup* of the dressing over the tuna.

● Quarter the potatoes. In a large bowl combine potatoes, beans, green pepper, tomatoes, olives, and ½ *cup* dressing. Toss lightly to coat. Cover and marinate tuna and vegetable mixtures separately in the refrigerator about 4 hours.

● To serve, combine romaine and Bibb or Boston lettuce. Spoon lettuce mixture onto large salad plates. Mound tuna mixture on top of lettuce. Then arrange vegetable mixture around tuna. Garnish with anchovies. Pass remaining dressing. Serves 4.

**Fresh Tuna Salade
Niçoise**

Florida Haddock Salad

Cool, crisp, and refreshing describe this tarragon-orange salad.

12 ounces cooked haddock *or* tuna
2 oranges
3 tablespoons salad oil
2 tablespoons tarragon vinegar
¼ teaspoon dried tarragon, crushed
⅛ teaspoon pepper
1 clove garlic, minced
2 cups torn iceberg lettuce
2 cups torn spinach
1 small red onion, sliced and separated into rings
½ cup sliced radishes

● Break or cut fish into large chunks. (You should have about 2 cups.) Place the fish in a dish just large enough to hold the fish in a single layer.

● Peel oranges. Over a small mixing bowl, section the oranges, reserving *¼ cup* juice. Cover and refrigerate the orange sections till they are needed.

● For dressing, in a screw-top jar combine the reserved orange juice, oil, vinegar, tarragon, pepper, and garlic. Cover and shake well. Pour dressing over fish. Cover and marinate the fish in the refrigerator about 4 hours.

● For salad, in a large salad bowl combine lettuce, spinach, onion, radishes, and reserved orange sections. Add fish-dressing mixture to the salad. Toss lightly to coat. Makes 4 servings.

Romaine with Bass

Jicama (HEE-kuh-muh), found in the produce section of the supermarket, has a delicate flavor like water chestnuts.

12 ounces chilled cooked sea bass, cod, *or* shark
7 cups torn romaine
5 ounces jicama, peeled and cut into 2-inch julienne sticks (about 1 cup), *or* one 8-ounce can sliced water chestnuts, drained
½ cup pine nuts *or* slivered almonds, toasted
⅓ cup light raisins
¼ cup salad oil
¼ cup dry sherry
2 tablespoons white wine vinegar
1 teaspoon sugar
¼ teaspoon garlic salt
¼ teaspoon dry mustard
Dash pepper

● Break or cut the fish into large chunks and set the fish aside. (You should have about 2 cups.) In a large salad bowl combine the romaine, jicama or water chestnuts, about *two-thirds* of the nuts, and raisins.

● For dressing, in a screw-top jar combine salad oil, sherry, vinegar, sugar, garlic salt, dry mustard, and pepper. Cover and shake well. Pour dressing over romaine mixture. Toss lightly to coat. Add the fish, then toss lightly again. Sprinkle with the remaining nuts. Makes 4 servings.

Fish-Louis Salad in a Bread Bowl

⅓ cup mayonnaise *or* salad
  dressing
¼ cup thinly sliced green
  onion
2 tablespoons chili sauce
½ teaspoon lemon juice
¼ cup whipping cream
1 loaf unsliced round whole
  wheat *or* white bread
  (about 9 inches in
  diameter)
1 12-ounce package frozen
  split crab legs, thawed
8 ounces chilled cooked cod,
  halibut, *or* whiting
2½ cups torn spinach *or*
  romaine
1 small tomato, cut into 8
  wedges, then halved
  crosswise

● For the dressing, in a small mixing bowl stir together the mayonnaise or salad dressing, green onion, chili sauce, lemon juice, and dash *salt.* In another small bowl whip cream till soft peaks form. Then fold the whipped cream into mayonnaise mixture. Cover and chill dressing while preparing salad.

● For bread shell, insert toothpicks around top edge of loaf. Using the toothpicks as a guide, cut into, *but not through,* the loaf to form a cone. Remove the bread cone. Finish hollowing out the loaf, leaving a ¼-inch-thick shell. (Reserve the bread from the top and inside of the bread shell for another use.)

● Remove crabmeat from shells, then cut crab into bite-size pieces. Break fish into large chunks. (You should have about 1⅓ cups of fish.) For the salad, in a large bowl combine spinach or romaine and tomato. Pour dressing over spinach mixture. Toss lightly to coat. Add crab and fish, then toss lightly again.

● To serve, spoon spinach mixture into bread shell. Then cut shell into quarters. Makes 4 servings.

Making your bread bowl
For your bowl, you'll need to start with a round, unsliced loaf of bread. To make the bread shell, insert toothpicks around the top of the loaf in about a 5-inch circle. Then, using the toothpicks as a guide, cut into the bread loaf at a 45-degree angle to form a cone. (Do not cut through the bottom of the loaf.) Remove the cone from the loaf. Then pull out the remaining bread from the inside of the loaf, leaving a ¼-inch-thick shell.

Creamy Salmon-Potato Salad

Chill the salad for several hours to let the many wonderful flavors blend together.

5 medium potatoes (about 1¾ pounds)
½ cup chopped *or* sliced celery
1 2¼-ounce can sliced pitted ripe olives, drained
4 green onions, thinly sliced
1¼ cups mayonnaise *or* salad dressing
1 tablespoon Dijon-style mustard
1 tablespoon vinegar
2 teaspoons celery seed
½ teaspoon salt
1 pound cooked salmon *or* tuna
3 hard-cooked eggs, coarsely chopped
2 tablespoons diced pimiento
6 lettuce cups

● In a large covered saucepan cook potatoes in boiling water for 20 to 25 minutes or till just tender, then drain. Peel and cube the potatoes. Transfer to a large salad bowl. Add celery, olives, and green onions. Toss lightly to mix.

● For the dressing, in a small mixing bowl stir together the mayonnaise or salad dressing, mustard, vinegar, celery seed, and salt. Pour dressing over potato mixture. Toss lightly to coat.

● For salad, break or cut fish into large chunks. (You should have about 2⅔ cups.) Add fish, eggs, and pimiento to potato mixture. Toss lightly to mix. Cover and chill for 4 to 8 hours.

● To serve, if necessary, add a few tablespoons of *milk* to potato mixture and toss lightly to moisten. Serve potato mixture in lettuce cups. Makes 6 servings.

Pasta 'n' Salmon Toss

Serve croissants or corn muffins to complete this spinach-pasta-salad meal.

¾ cup medium shell macaroni *or* corkscrew macaroni
¼ cup salad oil
3 tablespoons lemon juice
2 teaspoons Dijon-style mustard
¼ teaspoon salt
⅛ teaspoon garlic powder
⅛ teaspoon pepper
8 ounces chilled cooked salmon
3 cups torn spinach
8 cherry tomatoes, halved
¾ cup sliced fresh mushrooms
1 tablespoon grated Parmesan cheese

● Cook pasta according to package directions, then drain. Place cooked pasta in a medium salad bowl.

● Meanwhile, for dressing, in a screw-top jar combine salad oil, lemon juice, mustard, salt, garlic powder, and pepper. Cover and shake well. Pour dressing over warm pasta. Toss lightly to coat. Cover and marinate pasta in the refrigerator for 2 to 3 hours, tossing mixture occasionally.

● For salad, break salmon into large chunks. (You should have about 1⅓ cups.) Add the spinach, tomatoes, and mushrooms to pasta-dressing mixture. Toss lightly to coat. Then add salmon and toss lightly again. Sprinkle with the grated Parmesan cheese. Makes 3 or 4 servings.

Spring Greens Salads

Don't wait till spring to sink your teeth into this salad. Use romaine or leaf lettuce when sorrel is unavailable.

⅔ cup mayonnaise *or* salad dressing
½ cup crumbled blue cheese
1 tablespoon milk
1 tablespoon lemon juice
Few drops bottled hot pepper sauce
4 cups shredded iceberg lettuce
2 cups torn sorrel, romaine, *or* red leaf lettuce
1 small cucumber, thinly sliced
2 cups torn spinach
2 avocados, seeded, peeled, and sliced lengthwise
1 8-ounce package frozen cooked shrimp, thawed
Snipped chives (optional)
2 hard-cooked eggs, sliced

● For dressing, in a small mixing bowl combine mayonnaise or salad dressing, blue cheese, milk, lemon juice, and hot pepper sauce. Stir till well blended. Cover and chill.

● For salads, place iceberg lettuce in strips down the centers of 4 dinner plates. Combine sorrel and cucumber. Place sorrel mixture on one side of the lettuce and spinach on the other side of the lettuce. Arrange avocado slices in a fan shape on top of lettuce. Mound shrimp on top of lettuce near avocado. Spoon dressing on top of shrimp. If desired, sprinkle with snipped chives. Garnish with egg slices. Makes 4 servings.

Seafood-Pear Salads

For a different look, arrange the pear slices in a fan shape.

4 medium pears, halved lengthwise and cored
Lemon juice
½ cup mayonnaise *or* salad dressing
⅓ cup plain yogurt
¼ cup finely chopped seeded cucumber
1 tablespoon finely chopped onion
Bibb lettuce *or* Boston lettuce leaves
12 ounces frozen crab-flavored fish sticks, thawed and cut into 1-inch pieces
¾ cup plain croutons
Watercress sprigs (optional)

● Chop 1 pear half. Brush cut surfaces of remaining pear halves with lemon juice to prevent browning.

● For dressing, in a small mixing bowl combine the chopped pear, mayonnaise or salad dressing, yogurt, cucumber, and onion. Cover and chill while preparing salads.

● For salads, line 4 salad plates with lettuce leaves. Slice remaining pears lengthwise. If desired, brush cut edges of pears with additional lemon juice to prevent browning. Arrange pear slices in spoke fashion on the plates. Mound fish pieces in the centers of the pears. Spoon dressing over fish and sprinkle with croutons. If desired, garnish with watercress sprigs. Serves 4.

Gingered Shrimp Salads

Bias slice carrots and celery by holding the knife at a 45-degree angle.

1½ pounds fresh *or* frozen
      large shrimp in shells
¾ cup salad oil
¼ cup white wine vinegar
2 tablespoons water
½ teaspoon finely shredded
      lemon peel
1 tablespoon lemon juice
1½ teaspoons ground ginger
1 teaspoon sugar
½ teaspoon salt
2 cups thinly bias-sliced
      celery
2 cups thinly bias-sliced
      carrots
2 cups radish sprouts, fresh
      bean sprouts, *or* shredded
      Chinese cabbage

● Thaw shrimp, if frozen. Peel and devein shrimp. In a large saucepan combine 3 cups *water* and ½ teaspoon *salt.* Bring to boiling. Add shrimp. Cover and simmer for 1 to 3 minutes or till shrimp turn pink, then drain. Cool shrimp until they are easy to handle. Cut shrimp lengthwise in half. Place in a plastic bag. Place bag in a bowl.

● For dressing, in a screw-top jar combine oil, vinegar, water, lemon peel, lemon juice, ginger, sugar, and salt. Cover and shake well. Pour *half* of the dressing over the shrimp. Close bag and marinate in the refrigerator for 6 hours or overnight, turning bag occasionally. In another plastic bag place celery and carrots. Set bag in another bowl. Pour the remaining dressing over vegetables. Close bag and marinate in the refrigerator for 6 hours or overnight, turning bag occasionally.

● For salads, drain vegetables and mound them in the centers of 4 salad plates. Then arrange sprouts or Chinese cabbage around outer edges of plates. Drain shrimp. Lay shrimp, cut side down, in a circle on top of each vegetable mound. Serves 4.

Arranging the Gingered Shrimp Salads

It's easy to make these salads look elegant. First mound the celery and carrots in the centers of the salad plates. Then take your pick of sprouts or shredded Chinese cabbage and place it around the outer edges of the plates. (We used radish sprouts in the photo.) Finally, lay the shrimp, cut side down, in a circle on top of each vegetable mound.

Shrimp-Rice Ring

Quick-thaw the frozen shrimp and peas by placing them in a colander and running cold tap water over them.

1¼ cups mayonnaise *or* salad dressing

3 tablespoons chopped sweet pickle

3 tablespoons white wine vinegar

2 tablespoons milk

1½ teaspoons prepared mustard *or* Dijon-style mustard

1⅓ cups long grain rice

2 6-ounce packages frozen cooked small shrimp, thawed

½ of a 10-ounce package (about 1 cup) frozen peas, thawed

1 small tomato, peeled, seeded, and chopped

½ cup chopped fresh mushrooms

½ cup chopped celery

½ cup thinly sliced green onion

¼ cup salad oil

2 tablespoons white wine vinegar

½ teaspoon sugar

½ teaspoon salt

Leaf lettuce

1 medium tomato, cut into wedges

● For sauce, in a small mixing bowl combine mayonnaise or salad dressing, pickle, 3 tablespoons wine vinegar, milk, and mustard. Stir till well blended. Cover and chill.

● Cook rice according to package directions. In a medium mixing bowl combine hot rice, shrimp, peas, chopped tomato, mushrooms, celery, and onion. Set rice mixture aside.

● In another small mixing bowl combine salad oil, 2 tablespoons wine vinegar, sugar, and salt. Stir till well blended. Stir *½ cup* of the sauce into the oil-vinegar mixture, then pour it over the rice mixture. Toss lightly to mix. Press rice mixture firmly into a lightly oiled 6½-cup ring mold. Cover and chill for 6 hours or overnight.

● To serve, line a platter with lettuce leaves. Invert mold onto platter. Give the mold a sharp tap, then lift mold off. (If necessary, wrap a warm dish towel around mold to loosen salad from mold.) Garnish with tomato wedges. Serve remaining sauce separately. Makes 6 servings.

Curried Seafood Salad

Curry powder is not a single spice but a blend of many spices.

¼ cup tarragon vinegar
1 tablespoon honey
1½ to 2 teaspoons curry powder
⅓ cup salad oil
5 cups torn Bibb lettuce *or* Boston lettuce
3 cups torn spinach
1 cup sliced celery
½ of a cucumber, sliced
1 8-ounce package frozen cooked shrimp, thawed
1 6-ounce package frozen crabmeat, thawed and drained
½ cup coconut, toasted
½ cup slivered almonds, toasted
½ cup raisins

● For dressing, in a blender container combine vinegar, honey, and curry powder. Cover and blend for 5 seconds. Through the opening in the lid or with lid ajar, and with blender on slow speed, *gradually* add oil in a thin stream. (When necessary, stop blender and scrape sides.) Cover and blend till thickened. Cover and chill dressing.

● In a very large mixing bowl combine Bibb or Boston lettuce, spinach, celery, cucumber, shrimp, and crabmeat. Pour the dressing over lettuce mixture and toss lightly to coat.

● Immediately transfer mixture to a large salad bowl. Pass coconut, almonds, and raisins to sprinkle on individual servings. Makes 6 servings.

Gazpacho Salad with Shrimp

4 medium tomatoes, each cut into eight wedges
1 medium cucumber, thinly sliced
1 8-ounce package frozen cooked shrimp, thawed
1 medium green pepper, coarsely chopped
½ cup sliced celery
⅓ cup coarsely chopped onion
3 tablespoons snipped parsley
⅓ cup red wine vinegar
¼ cup salad oil
2 cloves garlic, minced
½ teaspoon salt
¼ teaspoon ground cumin
Few drops bottled hot pepper sauce
Dash pepper
4 Bibb lettuce *or* iceberg lettuce cups
Plain croutons

● In a large mixing bowl combine tomatoes, cucumber, shrimp, green pepper, celery, onion, and parsley.

● For dressing, in a screw-top jar combine vinegar, oil, garlic, salt, cumin, hot pepper sauce, and pepper. Cover and shake well. Pour over tomato mixture and toss lightly to coat. Cover and chill for 2 to 3 hours, lightly tossing mixture occasionally.

● To serve, using a slotted spoon to drain, spoon tomato mixture into lettuce cups. Top with croutons. Makes 4 servings.

Curried Seafood Salad

Bulgur Salad in a Pocket

Here's one for all you nut lovers. Peanuts, bulgur, and wheat germ give this hearty sandwich a delicious flavor.

  1 cup boiling water
  2 teaspoons instant chicken
      bouillon granules
  ½ cup bulgur wheat
  1 8-ounce carton plain yogurt
  ¼ cup mayonnaise *or* salad
      dressing
  ¼ teaspoon curry powder
  1 small apple, cored and
      chopped
  ½ cup coarsely chopped
      peanuts
  ½ cup wheat germ
  ⅓ cup sliced celery
  ⅓ cup raisins
  4 large pita bread rounds,
      halved crosswise
      Leaf lettuce

● In a medium mixing bowl combine boiling water and chicken bouillon granules, stirring till granules are dissolved. Stir in bulgur and let stand for 20 minutes. Drain well, then squeeze out excess liquid. Set bulgur aside.

● In a medium mixing bowl combine yogurt, mayonnaise or salad dressing, and curry powder. Stir till well blended. Add the drained bulgur, apple, peanuts, wheat germ, celery, and raisins. Toss lightly to coat. Cover and chill for 1 to 2 hours.

● To serve, line the insides of pita halves with lettuce leaves. Spoon bulgur mixture into the pita halves. Makes 4 servings.

Egg-Chard Toss

You'll find Swiss chard packs more of a bite than spinach.

  1 8-ounce carton plain yogurt
  2 to 3 teaspoons prepared
      horseradish
  1 teaspoon sugar
  ½ teaspoon salt
      Dash bottled hot pepper
      sauce
      Milk
  4 cups torn spinach
  4 cups torn Swiss chard*
  4 ounces cheddar cheese, cut
      into 1-inch julienne sticks
  1 cup cherry tomatoes, halved
  ¼ cup sliced green onion
  4 hard-cooked eggs, sliced

● For dressing, in a small mixing bowl combine yogurt, horseradish, sugar, salt, and hot pepper sauce. Stir till well blended. If necessary, stir in enough milk to make dressing of desired consistency. Cover and chill dressing while preparing the salad.

● For salad, in a large salad bowl combine spinach, Swiss chard, cheddar cheese, tomatoes, and onion. Toss lightly to mix. Add eggs. Pour dressing over spinach mixture. Toss lightly to coat. Makes 6 servings.

*If Swiss chard is unavailable, substitute additional spinach.

Tortellini and Parsley-Pesto Salad

1 cup lightly packed parsley
sprigs with stems
removed
2 teaspoons dried basil,
crushed
1 clove garlic
⅓ cup grated Parmesan cheese
or Romano cheese
¼ cup olive oil *or* salad oil
8 ounces broccoli
2 7-ounce packages cheese-
filled tortellini
1 2¼-ounce can sliced pitted
ripe olives, drained
6 ounces provolone cheese *or*
mozzarella cheese, cubed
2 medium tomatoes, seeded
and chopped
⅓ cup pine nuts, toasted, *or*
½ cup broken walnuts

● For pesto, in a food processor bowl or blender container combine parsley, basil, and garlic. Cover and process or blend till finely chopped. (When necessary, stop and scrape sides.) Add Parmesan or Romano cheese. Cover and process or blend till combined. With lid ajar, add oil a little at a time, processing or blending after each addition till well combined. Set pesto aside.

● Remove outer leaves and tough parts of stalks from broccoli. Cut the stalks crosswise into ¼-inch-thick slices, then break flowerets into smaller pieces. (You should have about 2½ cups total.) Set broccoli aside.

● In a large covered saucepan cook the tortellini according to package directions, adding the broccoli during the last 5 minutes of cooking. Drain.

● In a large salad bowl combine pesto, broccoli, tortellini, and olives. Toss lightly. Cover and chill for 4 hours or overnight.

● To serve, add provolone or mozzarella cheese, tomatoes, and nuts to the tortellini mixture. Toss lightly to mix. Serves 6.

Making parsley pesto
Pesto means "pounding" in Italian. Traditionally this sauce is made with a mortar and pestle. To simplify the method, use a food processor or a blender.

 Start with about 1¼ ounces of parsley sprigs. Remove and discard the stems. (You should have 1 cup of loosely packed parsley.) Place the parsley, basil, and garlic in a food processor bowl or a blender container. Cover and process or blend till finely chopped. If necessary, stop the processor or blender and scrape the parsley mixture from the sides of the container. This first step of processing is important to assure a smooth pesto.

Cheesy Apple Salad

You'll find Edam (EED-um) and Gouda (GOO-duh) cheese have a mild and nutty flavor.

3 tablespoons mayonnaise *or* salad dressing
3 tablespoons plain yogurt
1 teaspoon honey
¼ teaspoon celery seed
2 cups torn iceberg lettuce *or* spinach
2 small apples, cored and coarsely chopped
4 ounces Edam cheese *or* Gouda cheese, cubed
1 stalk celery, sliced
¼ cup broken walnuts

● For dressing, in a small mixing bowl combine mayonnaise or salad dressing, yogurt, honey, and celery seed. Stir till well blended. Cover and chill.

● In a large mixing bowl combine lettuce or spinach, apples, cheese, celery, and *half* of the walnuts. Pour the dressing over lettuce mixture and toss lightly to coat.

● Immediately spoon the lettuce mixture onto 2 salad plates. Sprinkle with the remaining walnuts. Makes 2 servings.

Three-Bean and Cheese Salad

Here's a south-of-the-border serving idea: Spoon this creamy bean mixture into the crispy tortilla bowls from the Taco Salad on page 10.

⅓ cup creamy buttermilk salad dressing
2 green onions, thinly sliced
¼ teaspoon dried basil, crushed
1 8½-ounce can lima beans, drained, *or* ⅔ cup frozen lima beans, cooked and drained
1 8-ounce can red kidney beans, drained
1 cup drained canned garbanzo beans
6 ounces Monterey Jack, cheddar, *or* Swiss cheese, cut into 2-inch julienne sticks
1 cup thinly bias-sliced carrots
½ cup sliced celery
Milk
Red leaf lettuce

● In a medium mixing bowl combine the salad dressing, green onions, and basil. Stir till well blended.

● Add beans, cheese, carrots, and celery. Toss lightly to coat. Cover and chill for 2 hours or overnight.

● To serve, if necessary, stir in a few tablespoons of milk to moisten bean mixture. Line a medium serving platter with lettuce leaves. Mound the bean mixture onto the platter. Serves 4.

Sizzling Cheese Salad

You choose which cheese to "sizzle" in the skillet. Gjetost (YED-ohst) has a sweet caramellike flavor; feta (FEHT-uh) has a sharp salty flavor.

1 egg
1 tablespoon water
2 tablespoons yellow cornmeal
1 tablespoon fine dry bread crumbs
1 tablespoon sesame seed, toasted
2 teaspoons grated Parmesan cheese
4 ounces Neufchâtel cheese *or* cream cheese, cut up
1 cup shredded gjetost *or* crumbled feta cheese
6 cups torn mixed greens
1 medium tomato, cut into 8 wedges
¼ cup pitted ripe olives
¼ cup salad oil
¼ cup tarragon vinegar
1 tablespoon thinly sliced green onion
1 teaspoon Dijon-style mustard
1 tablespoon butter *or* margarine
1 tablespoon cooking oil
4 small pita bread rounds, split horizontally and toasted

● In a small shallow bowl combine egg and water. In another small shallow bowl combine cornmeal, bread crumbs, sesame seed, and Parmesan cheese. Set the mixtures aside.

● In a small mixer bowl combine the Neufchâtel or cream cheese and gjetost or feta cheese. Beat with an electric mixer on medium speed till well combined. Shape mixture into 1-inch balls. Dip cheese balls into egg mixture, then coat with the cornmeal mixture. Flatten balls to form patties. Cover and chill for 1 to 2 hours or till patties are firm.

● Meanwhile, on a large serving platter arrange the mixed greens, tomato wedges, and olives. Cover and chill while preparing dressing and frying cheese patties.

● For dressing, in a screw-top jar combine salad oil, vinegar, onion, and mustard. Cover and shake well. Set dressing aside.

● To fry cheese patties, in a skillet heat butter or margarine and cooking oil. Add cheese patties. Cook over medium heat, carefully turning once, for 2 to 3 minutes or till golden.

● To serve, shake dressing and drizzle it over greens on platter. Arrange the cheese patties on top. Serve with toasted pita rounds. Makes 4 servings.

Egg Salad in Tomato Tulips

Great taste and fewer calories! Your egg salad will have both when you use yogurt and dry cottage cheese instead of mayonnaise.

 1 **cup dry cottage cheese**
 ½ **cup plain yogurt**
 ½ **teaspoon dried dillweed**
 ¼ **teaspoon salt**
 ⅛ **teaspoon pepper**
 4 **hard-cooked eggs, chopped**
 ½ **cup chopped celery**
    **Romaine leaves *or* alfalfa
       sprouts**
 4 **large tomatoes**

● For egg salad mixture, in a medium mixing bowl combine the cottage cheese, yogurt, dillweed, salt, and pepper. Stir in eggs and celery. If desired, cover and chill for up to 8 hours.

● To serve, line 4 salad plates with romaine leaves or arrange sprouts on plates. Cut out ½ inch of the core from each tomato. Invert tomatoes. Cutting from the top to, *but not through,* the stem end, cut each tomato into 6 wedges. Place tomatoes on the plates. Spread wedges slightly apart, then fill with egg salad mixture. Makes 4 servings.

Making tomato tulips
Choose large fresh tomatoes to make attractive cups for individual servings of salad. Make the cups by inserting the point of a sharp knife into each tomato near the core. Then cut out ½ inch of the core. Invert the tomatoes. Cutting from the top to, *but not through,* the stem end, cut each tomato into 6 wedges. Place tomatoes on the plates. Spread wedges slightly apart, then fill with the salad mixture.

Nut-Flavored Oil

A nutty aroma with the flavor of almonds, hazelnuts, or walnuts. (Pictured on page 45.)

1½ cups unblanched whole almonds, hazelnuts, *or* walnuts (about 7½ ounces)
2½ cups salad oil

● In a blender container or food processor bowl place nuts. Cover and blend or process till chopped. Through the opening in the lid, and with blender or processor on slow speed, gradually add *½ cup* of oil. Blend or process till nuts are finely chopped.

● Transfer nut mixture to a small saucepan. Clip a candy or deep-fat cooking thermometer onto the side of the pan. Cook over low heat, stirring occasionally, till thermometer registers 160°. Remove from heat and cool slightly. Combine the nut mixture with the remaining salad oil in a jar or bottle. Cover tightly and let stand in a cool place for 1 to 2 weeks before using.

● To use, line a colander with fine-woven cloth or a cup-shaped coffee filter. Pour oil mixture through the colander and let mixture drain into a bowl. Discard nut paste. Transfer the strained liquid to a 1½-pint jar or bottle. If desired, add a few whole nuts to the jar or label for identification.

● To store the Nut-Flavored Oil, refrigerate, tightly covered, for up to 3 months. Makes about 2½ cups.

Herb Vinegar

Just sprinkle on top of greens. This flavorful vinegar can stand alone.

2 cups tightly packed fresh herb leaves *or* sprigs (tarragon, thyme, dill, mint, *or* basil)
2 cups vinegar
Fresh herb sprig (optional)

● Pack 2 cups herbs into a hot, clean 1-quart jar.

● In a stainless steel or enamel saucepan heat vinegar till hot, *but not boiling.* Pour the hot vinegar over herbs in jar. Cover loosely with a glass, plastic, or cork lid till mixture cools. (The vinegar would erode metal lids.) Then cover tightly with the lid. Let vinegar stand in a cool, dark place for 1 week before using.

● To store the Herb Vinegar, remove herbs from jar. If desired, transfer liquid to a clean 1-pint jar or bottle. Either label or add an additional sprig of fresh herb to the jar for identification. Cover tightly with a glass, plastic, or cork lid. Place in a cool, dark place for up to 3 months. Makes 2 cups.

Orange Vinegar: Prepare the Herb Vinegar as directed above, *except* use *white wine vinegar* and omit the fresh herbs. Heat vinegar with three 3x½-inch strips *orange peel* (white membrane removed). Transfer hot vinegar and peel to a hot, clean 1-pint jar or bottle. Cover and let vinegar stand in a cool, dark place for 4 to 5 days before using. To store vinegar, remove peel.

Raspberry-Mint Vinegar

2 teaspoons dried mint, crushed, *or* four 3- to 4-inch fresh mint sprigs

½ of a 12-ounce package lightly sweetened frozen red raspberries *or* 1½ cups fresh raspberries

2 cups cider vinegar

1 cup dry red wine

● Place mint in a clean 1-quart jar. Set jar aside. Thaw raspberries, if frozen. (Or thoroughly rinse fresh raspberries with cold water, then drain well.) In a stainless steel or enamel saucepan bring the raspberries, vinegar, and wine to boiling. Boil gently, uncovered, for 3 minutes.

● Pour hot mixture over mint in jar. Cover; let stand in a cool, dark place for 1 week. Line a colander with fine-woven cloth or a cup-shaped coffee filter. Pour mixture through the colander and let drain into a bowl. Transfer the strained liquid to a clean 1½-pint jar or bottle. Cover tightly with a glass, plastic, or cork lid. Store in the refrigerator for up to 6 months. Makes 3 cups.

Basic Vinaigrette

½ cup olive oil *or* salad oil

¼ cup wine vinegar

1 teaspoon sugar

½ teaspoon salt

½ teaspoon dry mustard

1 small clove garlic, minced

● In a screw-top jar combine oil, wine vinegar, sugar, salt, dry mustard, and garlic. Cover and shake well.

● To store, refrigerate, tightly covered, for up to 1 month. (If you make the vinaigrette with olive oil, bring back to room temperature before serving.) Shake again before serving. Makes ¾ cup.

Tomato Vinaigrette: Prepare Basic Vinaigrette as directed above, *except* add ¼ cup canned *tomato puree* and 1½ teaspoons snipped *fresh basil* or *thyme, or* ½ teaspoon *dried basil* or *thyme,* crushed. To store, refrigerate, tightly covered, for up to 2 weeks. Makes about 1 cup.

Low-Cal Italian Dressing

This oil-less dressing has only 3 calories per 2-tablespoon serving.

2 tablespoons liquid fruit pectin

2 tablespoons finely chopped onion

¼ teaspoon garlic salt

¼ teaspoon dried basil, crushed

⅛ teaspoon dried oregano, crushed

⅛ teaspoon crushed red pepper

2 tablespoons cider vinegar

● In a small mixing bowl combine fruit pectin, onion, garlic salt, basil, oregano, and crushed red pepper. Stir in vinegar and ½ cup *water*. Cover and refrigerate overnight before using.

● To store, transfer dressing to a ½-pint bottle or jar. Refrigerate, tightly covered, for up to 3 days. Shake before serving. Makes about ⅔ cup.

Nut-Flavored Oil
(see recipe, page 43)

Raspberry-Mint
Vinegar

Tomato Vinaigrette

Low-Cal
Italian Dressing

Thousand Island Dressing
(see recipe, page 46)

Dill 'n' Chive Dressing
(see recipe, page 46)

Dill 'n' Chive Dressing

It's tangy, but so good! (Pictured on page 45.)

½ cup dairy sour cream
2 tablespoons white wine
    vinegar
1 teaspoon sugar
1 teaspoon dried dillweed
½ teaspoon salt
½ teaspoon dry mustard
1 small clove garlic, minced
⅓ cup salad oil
2 tablespoons snipped chives

● In a blender container or food processor bowl combine sour cream, vinegar, sugar, dillweed, salt, dry mustard, and garlic. Cover and blend or process for 5 seconds. Through the opening in the lid or with lid ajar, and with blender or processor on slow speed, *gradually* add oil in a thin stream. (When necessary, stop blender or processor and scrape sides.) Stir in chives.

● To store, refrigerate, tightly covered, for up to 1 week. Stir before serving. Makes 1 cup.

Thousand Island Dressing

Save 89 calories per 2-tablespoon serving by using reduced-calorie mayonnaise. (Dressing pictured on page 45.)

1 cup mayonnaise *or* salad
    dressing
2 tablespoons chili sauce
1 hard-cooked egg, finely
    chopped
2 tablespoons chopped dill
    pickle
2 tablespoons diced
    pimiento
1 green onion, thinly sliced
1 teaspoon prepared
    horseradish
    Several drops bottled hot
    pepper sauce
2 to 4 tablespoons milk

● In a small mixing bowl combine the mayonnaise or salad dressing and chili sauce. Stir in egg, pickle, pimiento, green onion, horseradish, and hot pepper sauce. Stir in enough milk to make dressing of desired consistency. If desired, cover and chill the dressing before serving.

● To store, refrigerate, tightly covered, for up to 1 week. Stir before serving. Makes 1⅔ cups.

Buttermilk Dressing

Check your buttermilk carton for the expiration date. That's how long this dressing will keep.

1¼ cups mayonnaise *or* salad
    dressing
¾ cup buttermilk
1 tablespoon snipped chives
¼ teaspoon salt
¼ teaspoon onion powder
¼ teaspoon garlic powder
⅛ teaspoon white pepper

● In a mixing bowl combine mayonnaise or salad dressing and buttermilk. Stir till well blended. Stir in chives, salt, onion powder, garlic powder, and pepper. Cover and chill before serving.

● To store, refrigerate, tightly covered. Stir before serving. Makes 2 cups.

Peppy Salad Dressing

Fruit pectin, typically used to thicken jams and jellies, gives dressing body without using oil.

1 tablespoon powdered fruit pectin
1 teaspoon sugar
⅛ teaspoon dry mustard
⅛ teaspoon pepper
¼ cup water
1 tablespoon vinegar
1 small clove garlic, minced

● Combine pectin, sugar, mustard, and pepper. Stir in water, vinegar, and garlic. Cover and chill for 1 hour. Chill to store two or three days. Makes about ½ cup or 8 (1-tablespoon) servings.

Herbed Salad Dressing: Prepare Peppy Salad Dressing as above, *except* add ⅛ teaspoon dried *basil*, crushed, and ⅛ teaspoon *paprika* to the dry pectin mixture. Continue as directed.

Parmesan Salad Dressing: Prepare Peppy Salad Dressing as above, *except* add 1 tablespoon grated *Parmesan cheese* and ¼ teaspoon dried *oregano,* crushed, to the dry pectin mixture. Continue as directed.

Creamy Onion Dressing: Prepare Peppy Salad Dressing as above, *except* increase the sugar to *1 tablespoon* and stir in ¼ cup sliced *green onion* and ¼ cup plain *low-fat yogurt* with the water. Continue as directed.

Orange-Poppy Seed Dressing

1 8-ounce container plain low-fat yogurt
1 tablespoon honey
1 tablespoon frozen orange juice concentrate, thawed
1 teaspoon poppy seed
1 teaspoon finely shredded orange peel

● Stir together yogurt, honey, orange juice concentrate, poppy seed, and orange peel. Cover and chill to store. Makes about 1 cup or 16 (1-tablespoon) servings.

Honey-Mustard Dressing

1 8-ounce container plain low-fat yogurt
1 tablespoon honey
1 tablespoon Dijon-style mustard
⅛ teaspoon pepper

● In a small bowl stir together low-fat yogurt, honey, mustard, and pepper. Cover and chill to store. Makes about 1 cup or 16 (1-tablespoon) servings.

Index